Lions

Laura Marsh

NATIONAL GEOGRAPHIC

Washington, D.C.

For Andrew—L.F.M.

The publisher and author gratefully acknowledge the expert review of this book by Daryl Hoffman of the Houston Zoo.

Paperback ISBN: 978-1-4263-1939-6
Reinforced Library Binding ISBN: 978-1-4263-1940-2

Book design by YAY! Design

Photo credits

Cover, Daniel J. Cox/KimballStock; Top border of page (throughout), Ace_Create/iStockphoto; vocabulary box art, Billy Kelly; 1 (CTR), Frans Lanting/MINT Images/Science Source; 2, Art Wolfe/Science Source; 4-5, Carl D. Walsh/Aurora Open/Corbis; 6 (LOLE), Sue Green/Shutterstock; 6 (LORT), Wendy Shattil/Alamy; 6 (UP), Steve Winter/National Geographic Creative; 7 (UP), shapecharge/iStockphoto; 7 (CTR), Eric Isselée/Shutterstock; 8, Eric Isselée/Shutterstock; 9, Jak Wonderly; 10 (CTR), Jeff Mauritzen; 11, Images of Africa Photobank/Alamy; 12 (UP), Michael Nichols/National Geographic Creative; 12 (LO), Michael Nichols/National Geographic Creative; 13, Michael Nichols/National Geographic Creative; 14-15, GlobalP/iStockphoto; 16-17 (LOCTR), Frans Lanting Studio/Alamy; 17 (LORT), Pal Teravagimov/ShutterPoint Photography; 17 (UPRT), john michael evan potter/Shutterstock; 18-19 (CTR), Michel Denis-Huot/Hemis/Corbis; 19 (RT), Ariadne Van Zandbergen/Getty Images; 20 (LE CTR), Jeff Mauritzen; 20 (UPRT), gresei/Shutterstock; 20-21 (BACK), LucynaKoch/iStockphoto; 20 (LO), Theo Allofs/Corbis; 21 (LORT), Mohamed Zai/Shutterstock; 21 (CTR LE), Eric Isselée/Shutterstock; 21 (RT), blickwinkel/Alamy; 21 (UPLE), jurra8/Shutterstock; 22-23, Michael Nichols/National Geographic Creative; 24-25, Gillian Lloyd/Alamy; 26, Eric Isselée/Shutterstock; 27 (LE CTR), Eric Isselée/Shutterstock; 27 (UPRT), Eric Isselée/Shutterstock; 28-29, Hal Beral/Corbis; 30 (RT), Jeff Mauritzen; 30 (LE), Michael Nichols/National Geographic Creative; 31 (LORT), Jeff Mauritzen; 31 (UPRT), Barcroft Media/Getty Images; 31 (UPLE), Art Wolfe/Science Source; 31 (LOLE), Dr. P. Marazzi/Science Source; 32 (LORT), Michael Nichols/National Geographic Creative; 32 (UPRT), George Mobley/National Geographic Creative; 32 (UPLE), Mary Beth Angelo/Science Source; 32 (LOLE), Jeff Mauritzen

National Geographic supports K–12 educators with ELA Common Core Resources.
Visit natgeoed.org/commoncore for more information.

Printed in the United States of America
14/WOR/1

Table of Contents

What Am I?

I am King of the Beasts.
And I like a big feast.

I rest most of the day,
but I like to play.

My legs number four.
Do you want to know more?

I . . . *roaarrrrrr!*
What am I?

A lion!

Big Cats

Lions are part of a group called big cats. Tigers, leopards, and jaguars are big cats, too.

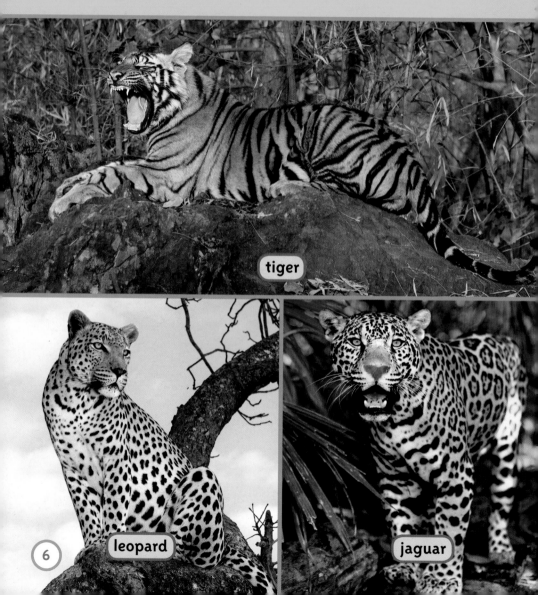

tiger

leopard

jaguar

How big are lions? They are much heavier than you! One lion can weigh more than three men.

All lions are big. But they don't all look the same. Male lions have a mane.

Female lions don't have a
mane. They are also smaller
than males.

Lion Around

Most lions live on the savanna (suh-VAN-uh) in Africa. It is very hot and dry there.

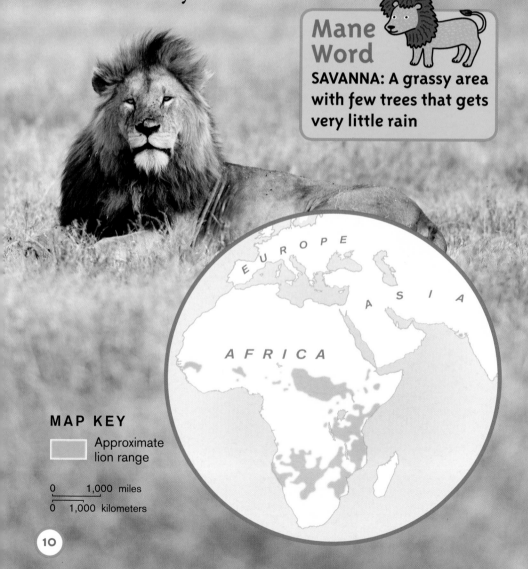

Mane Word

SAVANNA: A grassy area with few trees that gets very little rain

EUROPE

ASIA

AFRICA

MAP KEY

Approximate lion range

0   1,000 miles

0   1,000 kilometers

Lions need to rest to stay cool.
They lie in the shade. They also
climb trees to find a breeze.

Lions live in a family group called a pride. A pride can be as large as 40 lions. The pride rests, plays, and hunts together.

Super Hunters

Lions are meat-eaters. They eat other animals, or prey. A lion's body is built for hunting.

Mane Word

PREY: An animal that is eaten by another animal

TAIL: A long tail helps a lion balance as it runs and turns.

LEGS: Strong muscles help a lion run, crouch, and pounce.

EARS: They can hear prey more than a mile away.

EYES: Lions see well in the dark. They can easily spot prey at night.

TONGUE: A super-rough tongue pulls meat off a bone.

TEETH: Sharp teeth cut meat.

CLAWS: Sharp claws grab prey and hold on.

Lions usually hunt at night. It's cooler when the sun goes down.

Females do most of the hunting. They often hunt in a group.

Female lions hunting

Your favorite food might be pizza. But zebras and wildebeests (wil-dih-beests) are a lion's favorite foods!

zebra

wildebeest

Food Fight

Lions might be good hunters. But they are not good at sharing.

The adult males eat first.
Then the adult females eat.
The youngest lions eat last.
Sometimes there is not enough.
They often fight over food.

7 Cool Facts About Lions

1

They can eat up to 60 pounds in one meal. That's about 240 hamburgers!

2

Lions are the only big cats with a mane.

3

Most pet cats won't go in the water. But lions do. They may jump in to get their prey.

4

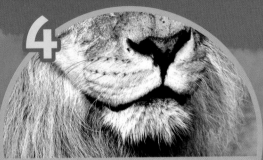

Spots around a lion's mouth make a pattern. Each lion's pattern is different. You can tell lions apart this way.

5

Lions keep their claws sharp by scratching trees, just like pet cats do.

6

A lion's tongue has tiny spines that face backward. The spines help a lion remove meat from bones and dirt from its fur.

7

A lion's roar can be heard five miles away.

Cubs

Baby lions are called cubs. They are born in a den. There they stay safe from other animals. The mother keeps them hidden for a few weeks.

The cubs grow bigger. Then they join the pride.

Mane Word

DEN: A hidden place in the bushes or a cave

It's playtime!

Cubs love to run, jump, and wrestle (RES-ul). They stalk and pounce.

Mane Word
STALK: To secretly follow something to catch it

The cubs play with almost anything, even mom's tail!

Playing helps the cubs learn to be hunters.

Lion Talk

Young lions also learn how all lions "talk" to one another.

A hum or a puff says "Hello." A snarl means "Back off!" And a roar means "Stay off my land!"

Hello.

Lions tell each other they are happy. They snuggle and rub heads. They lick each other, too.

Lions in a pride like to be together. They help one another live on the hot, dry savanna.

What in the World?

These pictures are close-up views of lions. Use the hints below to figure out what's in the pictures.

Answers are on page 31.

HINT: A family group of lions

HINT: Only male lions have this.

WORD BANK

cubs   teeth   claws   **mane**   tongue   pride

HINT: A name for lion babies

HINT: Lions hold down prey with these.

HINT: It helps a lion clean its fur.

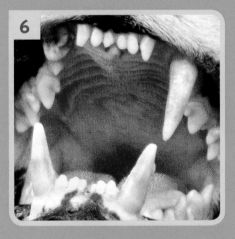

HINT: They cut meat.

Answers: 1. pride, 2. mane, 3. cubs, 4. claws, 5. tongue, 6. teeth

DEN: A hidden place in the bushes or a cave

PREY: An animal that is eaten by another animal

SAVANNA: A grassy area with few trees that gets very little rain

STALK: To secretly follow something to catch it